Soul-Searching

A Reflection of
Life, Loss, Longing, and Love

Renatta Lynn

Published by: Just Blessed Enterprises, LLC.
www.justblessedenterprises.com

Editing provided by: His Lighthouse Publishing Co

Connect with the author: Renatta@justblessedenterprises.com

ISBN: 979-8-9923129-0-4

Prelude

Out of the depths of my heart, in the spirit of transparency, may my poetry be a written testimony of the faithfulness and guidance of my Lord.

About the Author

Renatta Lynn began writing from an early age. She finds the art of written expression to be a valuable language used to speak on the most important issues and that writing provides an outlet for creativity. Even in her profession as an educator, Renatta Lynn lovingly instilled the significance of writing to her students through her motto, "If it isn't written, it didn't happen."

Over the years, she has been blessed with several opportunities to share her talent. She was a self-help columnist and celebrity interviewer for JO Magazine, Dayton, OH. She is also a contributing author for "And He Still Sees," "And He Still Waits," and "Seven Ingredients to an Effective Prayer Life *Volume 7*," published by Daughters of Distinction, LLC. In 2020, she released her first children's book entitled, "The Easter Skunk."

Presented for you now is a collection of poetry from Renatta Lynn's archives, *"Soul-Searching: A Reflection of Life, Loss, Longing, and Love."*

Table of Contents

Acknowledgements

Jesus,

I thank You for truly being the Rock of my Salvation. Without You in my life surely the darkness of life would have overwhelmed me.

To my mom, Linda (a.k.a. Lynn),

Mom, we share so much. We laugh and cry together. I am thankful for the time we have had to better understand our similarities and appreciate our differences. You stood by me and covered me in some of my darkest moments. Not surprisingly, you were often the first to rejoice with me in my victories and accomplishments. I am grateful for our friendship. I am blessed that God restored our relationship. I love you Mommy.

To my husband and children,

Our story is not like every other story, but I am thankful for God's redemptive and healing work. My family is my heartbeat, and I love you all.

Introduction

Soul-searching is an introspective look of one's conscience. It is a process of questioning and reasoning that can span a lifetime.

Throughout my life, I have wrestled with feelings of inadequacy, depression, and other internal struggles. Oftentimes, these struggles were magnified by external forces. From an early age, I was taught that prayer, faith, and God's word were the necessary tools that would ensure the salvation of my soul. Yet, my soul was searching.

Eventually, I retreated to silence. Whenever problems arose, I put on a brave face and refused to acknowledge my true feelings. I almost suffocated. How could I pray when I had no words? How can I believe when everything around me is seemingly falling apart? How can I read when my eyes are holding back tears and my mind is racing? I needed another tool to help me release the emotions and thoughts I could not verbalize. So, I found my solace in writing.

My fellow soul-searcher, I invite you to join me in these unspoken sentiments. I pray that my words can bring light to areas in your life that you have been unable to connect to. I encourage you to allow yourself to dive deeper into a space of reflection and release. Please use the reflection spaces following each section to write as you connect.

I present to you a portion of my struggles. I grant you a sneak peek into a journey through depression and oppression into the process of restoration in Jesus Christ. This is a soul's search through life, loss, longing, and love. Welcome to the voyage.

Life

Prayer of Gratitude

Dear Lord,

     I understand the joy of your heart as our Father is to be surrounded by Your children. There is no better moment than to awaken each day and see those precious faces and reflect on where they have come from.

     It was not long ago that I carried each of my children (these gifts) in my womb anticipating their births. Similarly, we were embedded in Your mind's eye. Heavenly Father, You watch us in wonder with deep intention to witness our coming forth and walking out our designated purpose.

     How truly grateful I am for each moment you have given to me. Help me to hold fast and remain focused. Help me to be in tune with every waking moment and to appreciate every breath.

     I will not carry what is not mine to carry. On the other hand, I will not let go of the gifts You have entrusted to me. I will align with Your divine will and purpose.

In Jesus' name,

Amen

December 14, 2020

My Sweet Little Angel

My sweet little one, all mine.
My own little angel, that came from inside.
You represent all the pureness of life
And are the reflection of the love I hold.
For you came from within
Reflecting my soul.

God gave me a ray of light.
You are all that has kept me.
Without knowing you I'd be lost having a dark end.
We bonded, and I told you my sorrows.
You listened intently and shared my pain.
And then hugged me from the inside out.

Even then, your whisper was not faint.
So long it has been before seeing your face
Now you are here in person
Here in this strange place.
So little angel, here I am and so are you.
I'll love you always and I'll always protect you.

Exact date unknown, 1998

Living in a Bubble

I'm just living in a bubble
Floating through life
From a daughter and a maid
to a mother and a wife.

I offend and pretend
laugh and cry
I feel hopeless, trapped
and don't know why.

I tried hard to change.
I really thought I had.
I feel so different.
Not quite happy, yet not sad.

I don't have a shoulder
I don't have a friend.
Only you by my side
On you, I depend.

I'm sorry, I plead
I'm sorry, I suffer
My heart still needs

Unintentional, yet hurtful.
Respect, yet disrespectful
I see now that my plate is too full.

Can I be this person I long to be?
Can I be a better version
of the soul that is me?

I try. God knows I do.
I never ever meant to hurt you.
I can't change it.
I don't know how.
I thought things would be different by now.

I know I messed up.
I see that I'm wrong.
Lord, help me
before it's too long.

I'm floating in a bubble
dazed and confused.
Someone tells a joke
I remain unamused.

Can I be this shallow?
This hollow image of a being?
Tell me the secret.
What is the real meaning?

I'm alone.
Yet, people surround me.
I feel like the choices I've made
have bound me.

Higher I bounce up to the sky
Seeking answers
I need to know why.

What will I be?
Where am I?
How can I change?
Why do I cry?

I feel like a monster,
maybe a beast.
My soul has such hunger.
Where shall I feast?

My life seems empty,
a dark and dreary path.
nothingness, despair,
anger, but not wrath.

I say to you, I'm sorry
and I love you so much.
But you do not acknowledge
It is me you will not touch.

A villain, a beast,
a creature alone
Seeking peace
Don't have a home.

It must end soon.
I must seek the way.
Today, will be forgotten.
Tomorrow, another day.

May 14, 2022

Confidence

Oh, it's you!

Come in. Take a seat over there.

Would you mind waiting for a moment?

I'm about to let down my hair.

Sometimes curly and sometimes straight

Nonetheless all mine. Real, not fake.

Oh, you like that, huh?

The way it hangs down to my waist

The sensual dark auburn brownness

Draped across my oval face.

And what about my face?

Oh, I am quite alright with it now.

You are shocked, aren't you?

You are thinking back to how…

I used to hate my image

My reflection reminded me too much

Of how often I'd been hurt

Self-infliction became a soothing touch.

My complexion is golden, yellow like sunshine

Ahh Ha Ha! You are staring.

Don't look too closely.

The brightness will leave you blind.

Oh no. Don't leave. I want you to stay!

I want you to recognize who I am today.

I found my purpose.

I found my place.

I am no longer clueless.

No longer do I feel like a disgrace.

Half of nothing; all of one Bi-racial beauty.

I blend in wherever, whenever I choose.

No longer a question of origin,

That game is over.

Guess what? You lose.

I've accepted my stature,

My shape and my skin.

After all, shouldn't I be comfortable with the package I'm in?

No, don't speak!

I've got much more to say.

I have had enough of the mind games you play.

You remind me endlessly of every fault and mistake.

That's why I took some time away.

I needed a break.

Now I have enough strength

To do what I must do.

I am totally finished with everything about you.

I don't need your pity.

I don't need your opinion.

I don't even want your goodbye.

I hold no animosity.

I wish you life and that's no lie.

You just can't live here.

There is no more room for you.

This is a party for one, not two.

You see… I learned the hard way,

I must love myself first.

Before giving away refreshment

I drink, because I thirst.

And no, I'm not selfish.

It's a survival technique.

This is love of myself -- all things unique.

November 23, 2010

Sometimes

Sometimes I feel like I can conquer it all.
Sometimes I feel like I am ready to fall.
Sometimes I am alone with no one to call.

My quiet, dismal hopes and raging fears cannot be contained by
a single encouraging word or touch.
Not this time.

Sometimes I feel like I'm not doing enough.
Sometimes I feel strength, I feel tough.
Sometimes the road is just too rough.

With one day, my perspective changes and all my ambitions
seem to go out the door.
Within hours my thoughts are redirected, and my happiness
returns to me once more.

Sometimes I wonder how long I can endure.
Sometimes my faith increases, and I am so sure.
Sometimes all falters into corruption and nothing seems pure.

Sometimes it occurs too often and always seemingly never
enough.
But perhaps sometimes it should be comforting.

After all, sometimes it is better than never unless the word and context come together to reveal uncertainty.

Sometimes, Sometimes, Sometimes...

February 17, 2013

Destiny

Almost got caught slipping. Almost got stuck looking back.
I thought temporary was forever and almost forfeited the
promise for a glimpse of fantasy.
But through it all you stood by me. You held my hand and
guided me to this point.
Lifted me up out of the valley so I could see higher than the
mountains.

I see the visions of heaven and the sun is shining brightly. Take
me to those better places and help me cast away the fears.
I walked in doubt but now I am free to soar higher. No more
shackles holding me down.
My arms raised high; my feet are lighter than air. Destiny is
calling.

Shadows overtook me. I was feeling through the dark for the
key.
Not knowing I possessed the lock, and the code was already set.
It was so simple I almost forgot.
Why stay in the closet when the door is open? I hid from my
failure when I should have embraced the victory.

Each ending offers another beginning, another chapter, another
opportunity for the plot to twist, shift and rise.

Amazing, the truth is light. Even when it causes anguish, the pain is reality, but so necessary for healing.
So, I embrace the process. I admire my scars. Knowing I am nearer to destiny.

Trip but don't fall. Fall but don't stay down. Wipe the dust. Take off running closer with each mile.
Out of breath, pace it. Breathe deeply. Echoes of purpose motivated.
Reminders of who I am. Why I am created. There is destiny.

June 1, 2022

Reflections

_____

_____

_____

_____

_____

_____

_____

_____

_____

_____

_____

_____

_____

_____

_____

_____

_____

_____

Loss

Prayer of Desperation

Dear Lord,

I really don't feel like I can endure much more of this situation. I sit here in silence, attempting to hold my tongue. I wish not to speak out in anger or ignorance caused by rage. However, I can only believe You will hold true to Your continuous reassurances. Prayerfully, I shall never endure this situation again.

Lord, help me to hold true to the victory given to me by You. Help me walk and talk according to Your likeness. My flesh is weak, but my spirit is strong, because I do embrace Your countenance. More of You and less of me. God mend me and mold me into a creature of happiness.

I seek to reap the blessings of salvation. Isn't joy one of these? What of continuous peace? I am holding my peace. I thank You for the strength to overcome murmurings.

I know You love me. But there are no buts. YOU love me and know what is best for me. You would never put more on me than I can bear. So, strengthen me. The end of this season has come. Let me not despair in the final moments. For this battle is not mine but Yours.

Faith, give to me Faith. Is this a test of my Faith? It must be. Am I passing? Am I pleasing? Wilt thou reward me? Yes,

You will. For I have suffered in silence and worked quietly. Thus, the Bible says, I shall be rewarded openly.

Increase, Increase. Enlarge my territory. Bless me indeed. I write You this prayer, because I sit here unable to extend these words to You. My mouth is bound up, by sorrow.

Jesus! Jesus! Jesus! Your precious name. I plead the blood of Jesus over this situation, over my family, over illness, over depression, over financial oppression. Break through! Break through! Break though! Lord, I love You and in You I put my trust.

In Jesus' name,

Amen.

November 27, 2007

A Poem of Encouragement

To: My Friends

Most do not believe
When a miracle has been conceived
All children are HIS
He loans them to us for a season
Their time here may be shortened
For whatever reason
Sometimes the sacrifice seems too great
Sometimes it seems Jesus comes too late
Rest in your faith
You did what most would not do
Now the glory of the Lord will pull you through
But just know that others have felt your pain
You are not alone in this time of rain
The sun is soon to shine
God will ease your troubled mind
He says, "Even I have lost a son."
"And for that sacrifice lost souls have been won!"
Therefore, smile and know there is a purpose
There is a reason
There is hope in HIM

August 2, 2008

Dedication to Daddy B.

Today, I cried.

I cried hard and loud.

There was no room to be proud.

I pleaded and begged.

I clenched my teeth in fear.

My face saturated with each descending tear.

I watched those who I thought were strong, scream and moan.

We really thought that tomorrow you'd be coming home.

I asked God "why," so many times.

His only answer was "because he's mine."

I wonder now; did we do enough?

Did we stick by you when things got rough?

Oh, please forgive us if we've failed you in any way!

We had no idea you'd be leaving today.

My heart breaks over and over again.

I lost not only a father figure, but the world lost a friend.

You always hugged me and smiled.

You always missed me when I left for a while.

Without you, I fear no one else will understand.

You really are a very special man.

I wish in some way this did not hurt so much.

I wish that once again I could feel your touch.

As you move onto your next journey, I want you to know.

I love you very much, your memory I won't let go.

I love you, Daddy.

June 30, 2009

Remembering You Always

So, I started missing you again.

I saw someone and started to wonder why.

What happened?

I never really gave you a chance and I am so sorry.

Can you forgive me?

Can I ever bring you back? Probably not.

I can't bring myself to think about replacing you.

I can't replace you.

Please know that I did, do, and always will love you.

You are so special to me.

I get quiet sometimes and try to imagine

Your smile, how you would look today if you were here.

So special and yet I just threw you away.

How can I ever forgive myself for that mistake?

How can I act like it never happened when I know it did?

I can only hope that someday we will meet again.

And when you see me, you'll know who I am.

And when I see you, I'll know you.

When we meet next, there will be no regrets.

March 4, 2010

Exit - The Weight of Escape

I was careful when I made my exit.
I didn't make any noise.
I didn't tell my story.
I just walked out, quietly.
I carried my bags alone.

I asked for help but found none.
I crept out gracefully, so I thought.
I didn't say I was leaving
I didn't tell them why.
I carried my bags alone.

I didn't have time to plan.
I just knew I had to leave.
I didn't have time to think.
I just scurried off without a trace.
I carried my bags alone.

I left some things behind.
I didn't think it would matter.
I wasn't sure where to go.
I kept forgetting about me.
I carried my bags alone.

I had to get dressed.
I needed to cover up.
I wasn't really ready.
I had no one to trust.
I carried my bags alone.

I always feel this way.
I left without a trace.
I didn't tell anyone I left.
I didn't leave hints or clues.
I carried my bags alone.

I am always carrying what wasn't mine, but you put your stuff in my bags and now I'm left with all your junk. I am tired of covering up your mess. You left me to carry these bags alone.

August 24, 2024

Reflections

_____

_____

_____

_____

_____

_____

_____

_____

_____

_____

_____

_____

_____

_____

_____

_____

_____

Longing

Prayer for Help

Dear Lord,

I feel that You are breaking me down, but I know it is so You are built up. In my heart, I feel like crying. Help me! Heal me! Teach me! It is so, Lord!

I don't have hatred, but I am too sensitive. I am too aware. I know too much. I feel like Eve who tasted the forbidden fruit. I now wish I could return to who I was. But I know that Your will must be fulfilled.

God, I love You so much. I yearn to know You and trust You. Jesus, help me to be what and who You know I can be.

I am trying, but I am still weak. Strengthen me.

In Jesus' name,

Amen.

Date unknown

Am I Good Enough?

Am I good enough?
Will I ever be?
How can I please you
If you don't want me?

I try my best
To be better
I can't stop being who I am
God made me this way!

If you don't like what you see
Talk to him, don't debate with me
In his sight I am wonderfully made
Now argue with that.

April 7, 2007

A Dream's Passing

Come inside to a place where dreams end
A life of lies, broken hearts, and sin
A place where the sun never shines
Come inside to this place where all hopes die
A mind of tears, pain and shrieking cries

This is the place of flowing falls
This is the place of endless fears
Enter this place to withhold your pain
Live the life of identity changed
Come in if you wish that you live a lie
Enter the void of despair where all dreams die.

Date unknown

Lost Little Girl

Lost little girl, why do you stammer?
Head bowed down
Arms folded
Trust distorted
Hope lost

The rain drenches your garments, saturating your very being.
Yet a desert within overtaking
Pure despair unveiled

Lost little girl, why do you pout
Eyes squinched
Avoiding tears
Mouth swollen with a million words
Yet no one to hear

Sunshine is beaming upon your hair and the heat burns cold.
No, you can't feel. The numbness overtakes.
Lost little girl, where is your hope?

Can I offer you comfort?
Rest in my arms. Safety is assured.
Love covers you, not too hot or cold
And my heart shall dry your pain

Lost little girl, have hope.

Seeking Abundance

You honestly think I will keep playing this game with you.
How many times have you rejected me, how often have you
disregarded me.
To you, my feelings are disposable or don't even exist.

I keep trying and changing, shifting and redirecting.
Still, I have come up with nothing.
I am still in this by myself, and you don't even understand.
I am in a place of giving up and unless I get a sign from God
Himself; that is what I am going to do.

I wondered if leaving or staying would be the sin.
But I now see the sin is to ignore my existence as a person.
It is a sin for me to disregard who God has called me to be.

Do you care to try and stop me?
Are you finally going to know that I am serious?
Will you take those necessary steps?
That remains to be seen, but as for me my mind is made up.

I chose me.
I chose to live freely.
I chose to love all of life and everything God has blessed me
with.

I know who I am and that is fearfully and wonderfully made in His image.

If He meant for me to hurt like this, He would not have sacrificed His own life that I could live.

He came that I might have life and have it more abundantly.

November 16, 2010

My Open Wound

There is a place within me that is hurting.
Sometimes I can feel it and sometimes I can't.
I pray on it and it goes away for a while.
Then the pain comes back, almost laughing at me.
So, I pray again and I fast.
The pain goes away but that doesn't last.

Here it is, now it seems worse.
Pray harder and longer.
The pain comes back stronger and stronger.
What is this pain I feel?
It is a test of the spirit, but to my flesh it is real.
Now it's swollen, this spot and sore.

I am sick of it!
Now what can I do? I can't give in.
I start all over; I will pray and fast. Again, and again.
There is a process, a pain for every level.
But when you withstand you defeat the devil.

Is my wound gone? No not yet.
But I know I can handle it.
It must leave! It must go!

Why?

Because through the blood of Jesus Christ, I declare it is so!

November 25, 2008

Reflections

Love

A Prayer of Release

Dear God,

I think I am kidding myself. I have been in a relationship for a long time. I have been committed for a long time, but through it all I have found myself alone and longing most of the time. And now I am at the crossroads.

I am so willing to release this situation entirely. I want to be strong enough to move forward and say I don't need anyone by my side. But the fact is, I fear being lonely even though it is so familiar to me.

Still, I am determined to serve You and put Your kingdom first. If I seek Your kingdom first, You will give me the desires of my heart. Only You know better than I what those desires are.

I love You, Lord. I trust You. Comfort my heart, mind, and soul. Sustain me where I am. Fill me Lord so that I am whole.

In Jesus' name,

Amen.

April 20, 2011

Love Me for Me

I wanna be loved from the inside out
I need someone to understand when I holla and shout
I want a man who will love me more than the game
I desire to be called only by my name

Someone with no extensive connections
Someone who will not play with my affections
Kind and caring yet tough and sure
A man whose values and love are pure

Don't just tap on my butt when you pass by
Learn how to hold and comfort me before I start to cry
You've been holdin' out on me for a while
When you walk in the room, I don't even feel a smile

Every burden you have, I take
But when I need to talk, you won't even stay awake
Yet you can't understand how this makes me feel
You get mad when I'm upset, but I am keeping it real

I hope you realize before it's too late
That I'm the best friend you've got, not to mention your mate

May 3, 2009

Second Place

I am the second, not the first.
Am I the better or the worst?
Is this love a blessing or curse?
Turned upside down is the universe.
Here we go over this same stuff again.
I keep fighting and never seem to win.
I don't understand why the arguing.
Why does the drama keep continuing?

The first is still here,
Why am I?
Almost every day I cry.
Insecure, worthless in my own eyes.
More painless it would be to die.
You chose not to see how sly
The enemy is. You are such a guy.
More and more. The harder, I try.
No price on happiness, money can't buy.

Still the second…
That fact remains.
Every day I am tortured; it drives me insane.
My mind whirls around, like an airplane.
You'd think he'd be more humane.

But no, to wish is in vain.

What good does it do to complain?

After the apologies, still the stain

Of brokenness.

The tears fall like rain.

July 20, 2009

Unanswered Questions

Here's to wishing you'd go away but still wanting you to stay.
You don't have any words for me day after day.
I feel like you want me, but most times you don't.
Do you even like me?
In uncertainty, I keep up this charade.

Truth is I am tired and ready for change.
Change of pace, change of season, change of scenery
Change between me and you.
But when and how remains a mystery.
Will you ever see you? Will you ever accept the real me?

I can't continue to be this way.
Holding my breath day after day
Holding my breath because the words I can't say.
You won't accept them if I did utter
You would only point back to me.

When you enter the room gray clouds hover.
And I beam like sunshine trying to force my way through.
I need to see blue skies. I need to feel a breeze.
I need to believe.
Will you ever just let me be me?

March 2, 2021

Think of You

Dear Love,

Today the sun shined brighter than I believe it has ever shone before.
The wind blew like silk against my face, softly.
Almost as if it had never blown at all.
I listened to the melody of the birds.
I watched as flowers danced in the wind.
Soon, with the bow of the trees, the scene ended.

Clouds scattered across the sky, filling it with darkness.
The scene became that of a mild afternoon shower.
The rain trickled down like a tear down a lonely lover's cheek.
The rain quickly stopped, and the pain would soon end.
The soft glow of sunshine brought forth comfort.

Later, the horizon swallowed the sun as birds sang sweet lullabies.
Fire splashed across the sky.
Slowly the moon made known its power as it emerged from the fading flames.
Darkness rapidly engulfed the sky.
One by one, the stars appeared; racing across the night creating images of light.

A humming silence could be heard in the distance.
The stars twinkled at the moon as they danced throughout the
night.

As I witnessed the day turning, taking on the form of night,
I thought of you.
Just as the continuity of life, always.
When the sun awakens the night from its sleeping splendor,
As the dew glistens in the morning's glory,
When the moon and stars slowly fade into the bright fire of the
sun.

As birds sing melodies to the rhythm of the wind,
As the flowers and trees waltz in the magnificence of life,
At night when the sun's glory is silenced as it descends below
the horizon.
When darkness overcomes the light and night becomes a life,
I do and will forever think of you.

Exact date unknown, 1995

Reflections

_____

_____

_____

_____

_____

_____

_____

_____

_____

_____

_____

_____

_____

_____

_____

_____

_____

_____

Author's Final Thoughts

My fellow Soul-Searchers,

Thank you for participating in this portion of my journey. I pray you will be encouraged and strengthened as you continue in yours.

If there is anything I would offer, it would be this... When the challenges of life seem unbearable, keep moving. Find moments to rejoice and take notice of small victories. Don't get stuck in the past. Instead, hold fast to your growth and healing as you progress to the next life lesson. Finally, continue to press toward the goal for the prize of the high calling of God in Christ Jesus. (Philippians 3:14 *author's interpretation*)

Wishing you peace and blessings,

Renatta Lynn